SEALS IN THE INNER HARBOR

Books by Brendan Galvin

SEALS IN THE INNER HARBOR

Brendan Galvin

Carnegie-Mellon University Press
Pittsburgh 1986

ACKNOWLEDGMENTS

Thanks to the editors of the following publications for permission to reprint these poems:

Amicus Journal: "Poem of the Towhee"
Ascent: "Finbacks"
Georgia Review: "Night Ways"
Harvard Magazine: "The Knot Hole Gang"
Michigan Quarterly Review: "This Fog," "Robbing Clam Beds"
The New Republic: "Seals in the Inner Harbor"
The New Yorker: "Chickadee," "Old Woodsroads," "Weather Breeder,"
   "Warmth," "Pollen," "Willow, Wishbone, Warblers "
Palaemon Press Broadside Series: "Märchen"
Ploughshares: "Beachplums," "Rural Mailboxes"
Poet Lore: "Your New Dog"; "The Last Man in the Quabbin" won *Poet Lore*'s Narrative Poem Competition for 1984.
Poetry: "Whirl Is King," "Workout," "Black Bear in October," "Fall
   Squashes," "Fog Township," "Mayflies," "Pole Beans"
Poetry Northwest: "Those Times"
Quarterly West: "October Flocks"
Southern Humanities Review: "Mosquito Fleet"
Tar River Poetry: "Stone Arabia Farm," "Summer School," "Looking for
   Captain Teabag," "Town Pier Parking Lot," "Cougar"
Three Rivers Poetry Journal: "Listening to September," "Nests"
Tri-Quarterly: "Wreckers," "A Block Island Cowhorn," "Light from Fundy"

"Rural Mailboxes" and "Mosquito Fleet" were reprinted in *The Anthology of Magazine Verse & Yearbook of American Poetry — 1985* (Monitor Book Company).

Thanks also to the Connecticut Commission on the Arts, which helped with the completion of this collection by awarding the author a generous creative writing grant.

The publication of this book is supported by grants from the National Endowment for the Arts in Washington, D.C., a Federal agency, and from the Pennsylvania Council on the Arts.

Carnegie-Mellon University Press books are distributed by Harper and Row.

Library of Congress Catalog Card Number 85-71692
ISBN 0-88748-050-0
ISBN 0-88748-051-9 Pbk.
Copyright © 1986 Brendan Galvin
All rights reserved
Printed and bound in the United States of America
First Edition

811
GALVIN
64646

CONTENTS

For Carla and Peter

Warmth

One flick of the wrist
and heat from the baseboards
comes sneaping around your ankles
like the worthless, expensive
pet of a sycophant.
But for warmth that stands up to you
when you come in the kitchen door,
warmth tinged with coffee,
bayleaf, cloves, and stick cinnamon,
that drifts from the pot and meets you
face to face, you have to kneel
in blue, knuckle-popping cold
as in the oldest liturgy,
stiff-shouldered and shaggy
as any man any dawn, and petition
the four-legged iron belly of
the stove against the meniscus
of frost on every window. It takes
junk mail under sleeves of bark
and those shingle-thick
parings the axe sliced away
from knots tough as trolls' knees
to summon heat that tells February,
Move it! Quit dragging your heels!
and brings the hideaway milkweed bug
in his orange racing stripes
out of his log, to muse at
your windows and make you wonder
who else is out there
sleeping in your woodpile.

Chickadee

The crow is only an anvil,
and the goldfinches' song
can be duplicated by rubbing
the right sticks together.
Next to yours
the blue feet of titmice
are merely a fad.

There are jays with voices
full of elbows
in my world, too,
dragoons on leave,
who appear to have molted
all the way to their head points.

But you, minimal wingbeat,
you're there, not there:
the economy of your arrival
puts a whole squad
of evening grosbeaks to shame.

I believe that other puritan
was looking at you when
he first thought, "Beware of
enterprises that require
new clothes."

I've believed in your way
since that evening
the owl sat
waiting for light to drain
into dusk, and you
flew straight in

and, seeing him there,
at the last instant
dipped up just enough,
and taught me
the duende of chickadees.

Old Woodsroads

Sowed shut with humus
and scuts of moss,
with highbush overgrowth
and domestic canes,
severed by cul-de-sacs
and overlays of hillside,
cut and filled,

what's left of
Veenie's Road and Over & Down
are still the best places
to scare up
a different birdcall:

by day, to wonder what
makes the song that forms
like a perfect carafe
at the end of
a glassblower's rod,

and to hunt by night
for the marshfire
woodcocks circle, heads jodding
to the hollow log's
drumbeat, an event you'll hear

but never see, just as
you won't meet
the people these roads
bespeak, who were shy
of the unconsidered answer

and preferred these hollows
to heights, and the long way
around. Or in winter,
to follow the first flakes

when they tear themselves
through everything raw,
barbed, and abrasive,
not fooled by foundations
and fences, by "No
Trespassing,"

to lie in
the wrong places
and lift these old tracks
back to light.

Rural Mailboxes

The air can still inspire
a kind of tinny speech
down their whole strung-out
stagger. Late March,
and they're still awed
at the quick-freeze of winter.
Like a madman jawing to nobody
in sight, one's telling
how he keeps getting kidnapped.
Another's been hit-and-run,
the hubcap's here to prove it,
and a third, caught out
on Halloween, still dribbles
the surplus of harvest.
All were plowed
under ninth-wave heaves of snow
on this faulted road
that never planned the lengths
and widths it's gone to,
where later a man will come —
oddly driving the whole way from town
to shut them up, all but this one
who's lost his name and resembles
the house he waits beside. In him,
a month from now, two birds will build.

Fog Township

It's that delicate time
when things could spill
any way, when fog
rides into the hollows,
making bays, and Cathedral
and Round Hills are
high islands. Brooks
have already churned back
into their beds to trickle
their own placid names
again, and cloud shadows
have drawn across
the landscape's lightest
moments. Now I begin
to hear something trying
to come through, a message
tapped on twigs out there:
the spring genius of this
foggy township knitting up
cable and chain to bind
the acres, among moss stitches
laying down her simple
seed and fern stitch,
complicating the landscape
a pattern a day: daisy
stitches and wild oats,
berry knots interspersed
with traveling vine
and dogwood. Her needles,
cut from oak tips,
click like sparks fired

across a gap, and I
imagine her crouched on
a stump, hair wet, pulling
April back together.
But for the lethargy that's
floating in this fog
in nets so fine they can't
be seen, I might walk around
out there until I meet her,
or scare off the jay
who's chipping for sustenance
along a pine's gray limb.

Mosquito Fleet

Dockside, these draggers look like hope
scraped over and retooled:
the *Tinkabelle*, the *Harold & Dru*,
in fog so rich it's foreclosing
on the river and the slumped
baitshack and the plank bridge
into town. Forsythia by the doors
are meek effusions, golden agers
who know their volunteer work
isn't worth a damn
when undersea pressures won't release
the air. While the Weathermaker's
waiting around headlands, it's unwise
to stand full height. We keep
looking away from hunched
consultations, expecting a four-inch
snow, struggling for words
to nudge the hour hand around
and tap the bad current
off our voices. Spring after spring
on the water, it takes engines
straining at the drags, and hatchets
whacking oysters clear of rocks
to start a breeze shaking
sickle-winged birds from its folds,
unshuttering things at the tips
of twigs and sandspits. It takes
a wink in every word
to draw the splinter out of the price.

Mayflies

Years in the bottom scum
of local cow ponds,
wriggling free of former
selves, learning new ways
to breathe — till they rise
in unison before a dawn, unable
even to feed, between their brad
heads and split tail-hairs
new wings that drive
each female to charge
a wandering black cloud of
mates that looks as though
it could jam horsepower.

Under them frogs dance
and splay, tongueing air
to get up where birds
work the swarm's crackling edge
before its passion fails
to a carbon fall.

Let the great trees look down
and judge from their hill
above the school how close it comes
to the May evening
a cloud of color swirls
in that cafeteria.

Prom night: plenty inside
would tell you that school
and this one-cylinder town
are like life under water,
the whole cycle. But tonight,
trailing sherbet colors
and scents those colors might have
all over town, they seem taller

than last year, as around them
parents set off flashbulbs . . .

Here I will let analogies fail,
not say what mothers and fathers
and teachers are like,
but drop such connections into
the mind of Jimmy, town drunk,
where they will spin and grow wet,
leaves on a pool awhile,
which drift, sink, decompose as
he watches from those trees.

Finbacks

They say there's an evening
each June when the sea
between Wood End
and the great blue hill
of Plymouth is milk-calm,

and so many spouts
blow and hang on distance
it looks like Massachusetts Bay
is trying to grow a forest.

Humps flash briefly, like waves
catching and losing sun,
and all down the bay
finbacks are sliding
and sounding, so many

that even crabs
climbing the spilled midden
on a dragger's deck
seem to pause,

and soon, alongside,
the first whale rises
like a continuing wave,
and not exactly dives,
disinterested,

as lets the sea
close over its back,
leaving one gelid-looking pool
before rising again far on.

One by one,
hats come off
and the workboats
shut down: no squealing
winches, no Country-Western
from the radios.

Poem of the Towhee

Peripheral leaf-shufflers,
they're a black stroke of
the Japanese brush
over a reddish, quietly
passionate streak.
This one has bunted the window
all spring, baffled by glass,
and now, over my head,
a gray, humped spider has set up
like a text creeper
before the poem the towhee
printed there in accents
grave and acute, in characters
beyond any translation.

Sea Huns

1. *The Cook of the Tug Bayonne*

Two days later I'm on the train
to New Bedford, and my sea-traveling
times are done. Nobody shoots me
for swabbing the Hotel Picard lobby
or popping a rag over some gent's
shoes in the barber's. Some Knight
of the Camellia wants to try,
I can jump in the boiler room
or run for it. But out there,
bullets whanging around, air full of
toothpicks that used to be
the deck, nowhere to hide.
When that thing came up, rolling
water off its back, it was like
you're walking home past a weed field
every day and then one day
an elephant stands up next to you,
with only you in his eye.
Before that though, midsummer
Sunday morning, churchbells donging
over the ocean, soothing
the sea, low roll of fog cooling
the offshore. We were towing
four empties south to New York,
slow enough I could troll strips of
squid. Always fish chowder on,
when I'm cooking. Then that periscope
rose up. First I'm hoping they shoot
the kid, him up there waving
Old Glory, asking for it.
Next I was too busy dodging around
to think of anything. Good years,
they were, even with Slater
and the boys needling me, time-to-time.

I'm Cape Verdean, I tell them,
born right here in Acushnet, but that kid,
flag-boy, always in the way and saying,
"Jack Johnson's weak in the belly,"
saying we ain't got any nose bone.
Plenty of times I warned him, "Hey,
nice boy, I'll fix your biscuits."
Here's Slater in the picture,
Andrews, with his lodge pin still on,
Josh, me, McCargill, who lost that
funny hat, whole League of Nations
taped on my mirror, looking out to sea.

2. *Reverend Franklin*

I believed they were firing
at our very belfry,
such comminations the bells
seemed to be rending above
our heads. Only later did
the sexton confess to sounding
the alarm. My congregation
disbanded for the compass points
out doors and windows,
insects caught by the sun
beneath a stone, while I spoke
the Twenty-Third Psalm.
When I arrived at the bluffs
one barge was capsized
three miles out, and the *Bayonne's*
wheelhouse was gone.
No last prayers were required,
praise God, but those German boys
struck a mine off Europe,
never to make home port. It was
after the war I read of
the *Blechkoller*, how heat and

diesel fumes mingled with bilge
to coagulate hair and raise
mildew on jumpers and bunks, how
only a day out of Kiel
sausages would turn fuzzy as
caterpillars, and confusion
of night and day, coupling down there
with hellish engine noise,
drove suspicion to rage: the tincan
neurosis. One Easter I asked
that parish of sots and wifebeaters,
fishwives and sons of mooncussers,
to remember the souls of their
drowned enemies, and by Whitsun
was called elsewhere by my Bishop.

3. *"Stillson"*

I was sleeping Saturday off
in the squadron room when
the call came in. The boys were
up in P-town, playing the Coast Guard,
and since I turned dreamer when
things got slow in the outfield,
my mind lifting off the grass
and wobbling out into the blue,
crazy to be up there, and anyway
the ball, when it got near me,
always seemed to know how I'd move
and hop elsewhere — they must have
tiptoed out. Even now if I lean back
and shut my eyes I know how
it feels to climb out of humidity
and see heat rippling below,
then pick up a southwest breeze
under my tail, that cradle of struts
and wires dragonfly-light, and bank

towards the north. Up there my head
cleared quick, and the sea looked
slow and thick as jellyfish.
Off Nobscusset I caught the gray
sliver of a U-boat, its deck
cannons flashing a few seconds
before the sound reached up to me.
Back of the bluff cottages, sand
kicked up in sprays: those Hun-bastards
were lobbing three-inch shells
at Americans on vacation! The tug
was smoking, but by then all four
barges were under. Onshore they were
hauling survivors out of lifeboats,
and somebody seemed to be running
around wrapped up in a flag.
I was the American who got closest
to Von Oldenberg. Coming in low
out of the sun, I swear I could have
lifted his coal-hod helmet off
by the arrowhead on top, even
jerked him onto a wing by one end
of his schmutz of a moustache.
But why I took that particular
flying boat up — my brain must have been
cobwebs not to see no machine gun
was mounted and no eggs hung under
the wings. On the floor was a two-foot
wrench. I missed her by thirty feet
and they called me "Stillson" till the day
they mustered me out.

4. *The Boy Who Waved the Flag*

Did I think at the sight of it
they'd dive and bolt, or the sky
fill with rank on rank of
Nieuports, and backing them
a vision of rock-jawed doughboys,
George Washington in cloud-face
looking on above it all?
The crew was ducking and screaming
around Cookie, who knelt face down,
hands on his ears, praying to Mecca
in Portuguese. All hands saved,
they changed in the Bond Drive
poster to haggard women clutching
babies. Nearby an arm is reaching
from the sea where it bushes up
with shellfire, and from
a conning tower the Boche lean
cheering, a wolf pack dressed
in shadows. Heel-up, its rudder
in the air, the *Bayonne* is now
a tanker, its black soul
puffing from the funnel. When I
was photographed with Wilson,
I never asked him why just one
seaplane showed up late.
In the poster they made me look
about twelve, a scoutmaster's
afterthought, freckled,
pink-cheeked, blonde hair,
blue eyes, scout hat and neckerchief,
the flag too big — all wrong
the boy stood on the burning deck.

Town Pier Parking Lot

From the time we were caught up
in its drawn-out, shallow
flight dips and the way it used
masts for an overview, its silhouette
shifting like a wind pennant,
then dived, and flew to a crosstree
to swallow the catch, we must have
followed that kingfisher half an hour.
I was too tricked out in my new ego
to see events like this when I was
a kid here, my eyes so slicked over
with self I used to think
those couples who'd park at the pier
an evening and just sit still
were busybodies or so bored that
a dragger off-loading or fish truck's
departure for Boston was a thrill.
I was streamlined with talk then,
and they seemed already cracked
and peeling, but now that we're
nearly the age they were and can
call them by their Christian names,
I see how the world waits for us
to warp to its weathers and need it,
sends from its least places
a kingfisher, or in winter, as fog
takes the breakwater and draggers,
a heron flying in, just blue enough
to be separate from fog.

Pollen

As when a breeze
slips off the water
and crosses a headland,
and even those limp zeroes
wavelets make, fragile as
smoke rings, erase themselves
from the viscid surface,
and sails slacken,
so the air
this afternoon slackens,
and the page blurs
under your eyes
as the massive invisible
orgy of flower
quickening flower
sifts through the atmosphere,
drifts at its peak,
rose to rose,
and from roadside locust trees
birds stagger, drunk,
daring tires,
kneeling in the grass.

Insistent as midges, grains
tease at your nostrils,
and you cry onto the page
for no human reason.
And if somewhere
a boy's arm breaks the chains
of this lassitude
long enough
to toss a stone at a squirrel,
that pine exploding into gold
tilts you toward sleep
lightly. You whisper
how wings and the shadows of
wings circle you,
surrounding the years.

Wreckers

From a high dune
of the future, behind me
the radar domes like
broken puffballs,
I'll watch a torso,
then a whole man
materialize out of
that curtain of heat
up the beach, surf already
filling his footprints.
I don't want to think,
let alone have to dream,
what he's been through,
or to look into survival's
face as he unfolds and lays out
the cloth bag of tools
above the tideline, meticulous
as a surgeon, and kneels
to a beached shark-shape, finned,
vented, burnt-out, its dead brain
wired to eyes more unsparing
than any predator's. Tapping,
unscrewing a plate, how
will he use those parts
he's pocketing like trinkets?
Here, 1778, they divvied the crew's
greatcoats and blankets of good
English wool, then picked
H.M.S. Somerset down to her
mast wedges. "There's a very
plundering gang that way,"
General Otis said. Deckhouses
regularly turned hencoops,
and above a few trim capes
that still hide the Somerset's
ribs and planking under fillets
and clapboards, they're running
tests on the radar domes today,
racketing in so low
I look for crownfires in the pines.

Night Ways

Like rock-and-roll with headlights,
the last revelers have come back from town,
or a shower just passed,
millipede over your roof,

and now you're too alert to dive back
into that pillowing wave of unconcern,
not animal enough
to huff once from the belly,
expelling the whole day
as a dog can.

No. With skipping heart
you have to inventory
everything left outside
in the innocent light,
hoe, clam rake, clothesline,
anything that could be used
as a weapon,

because now each adjustment of the house,
as it stays up, recouping and settling,
finding ways to lean without
becoming ruins, is a predator's
single move, who has all the hours
of the sun's undertaking
to reach your bedside.

Stop this. As a heron concentrates
and slowly becomes the grass
surrounding a place of shallow water,
try hunkering down in your mind
by this beautiful, leaf-lined
Ojibway word: muskeg.

One at a time, without counting,
supply it a thousand
sphagnums and worts
to muse the edges,
and if all that green
doesn't draw you into its blur,

change rhythms: follow the motions
of swallows over it all,
blue-black as mussel shells,
turning to show
the mussel's orange belly.

Now, if a crow somewhere
has drawn the bent, eight-penny nail
of its voice
from a barn wall,
and you're still awake,
think of distances.

Far in those skies, seed-small,
a lone bird, vagrant off the tundra
and coming this way,
to wade this very muskeg,

as every day specks tumble
out of the wind,
to dirt and common water,
and since you have the time,
you may be just the one
to follow their unraveling
till wild asparagus
go to seed in your sleep.

That failing, when light's
first warbler finds its key
and begins turning it
in a rusty lock,
may you be traveling uphill
on some fire-road you almost know,

when above you something
you haven't thought of yet,
its rope tail and pelt
tuned to an angle of sunlight
in scrub, its spine an easy sway
between packed shoulders and rump,

looks back,
its mouth a slight downturn,
its green-yellow almond eyes
holding you in its dreaming regard.

This Fog

A bluefin may nose
up to a window, glum,
with an underslung lip,

if it keeps thickening
like this. Or jacks,
their eyes deeply troubled
by lamplight, passing
among morose,
hypodermic-looking schools.

When I wiped
my glasses this morning,
the smudges hung
on air like thumbprints.

Specks were floating
out there, and trees trapped
doghair swatches
you could card and spin.

By noon I felt like
the only thing alive
in an early daguerrotype.

Matchheads crumbled away
at a scratch; on the table
a bowl of apples
was sweating out
their decline into jelly.

The atmosphere slipped
into clothes
and rests under
my arms now,
solid as waterwings.

I wait for both feet
to lift from the floor
and stay there. Talk
is already
a protozoan scatter,

but I haven't panicked,
haven't yet seen
shapes with spiny
antennas, rhomboids
pressurized by the depths,

less like fish
than a child's drawing
of fish. These double
thermopanes
haven't yet shattered.

Märchen

Then, as we picked
raspberries so juicy
my shirt looked buckshot,
it seemed we hadn't watched
closely enough, and canes
that had surrounded
the house grew over it.

Had we read those homilies
against desire — bugs
who danced themselves
to silence on our sills
hunting a flaw in glass,
so many they could
fill a seed packet,

and the maple by the door
that grew cross-purposes
of angles with itself —
we might have known.

But we wanted that fruit
the way we wanted to be led
through the dark by
a branch of small green stars
plucked from a blur
of misted tree lights,

and now you're truly
the little woman,
I'm the little man,
each with the simpleton's
face of a dried apple doll,
and it's lovely in here,
with the sun relayed
from leaf to leaf.

When friends come to the
edge of our thicket and call,
we cry "It's a feast,"
and they go away, though
maybe to draw us out
someone has left
this baby by the door,
cradled in half a walnut shell.

A Block Island Cowhorn

When she came up the bay,
a squall of canvas over twin
bow and stern points,
a vessel the moon
would be proudly borne in,
stinkpots and floating dinettes
were doodlebugging around her
as if to apologize for two weeks
of leisure per year. Then I knew
we'd consigned angels to henyards
when we gave up sail. It was
as if Susannah were backstroking
across a farm pond, among
water beetles and whirligigs,
and I said "Flying Cloud"
from the diaphragm till my heels
involuntarily rose and the deck
under me rippled. I said
"Wild Hunter" and air hit
my blood like whiskey. "White
Squall, Wild Hunter, Flying
Cloud," and my cerebrum went
aloft in a sixty knot gale.
But "Dynafuel" and "Gypsum Queen"
I had to mumble into my teeth.
Quarterboard fleur-de-lis
wilted to dollar signs and the sea
calmed to miracle fibers.
Thresher and hammerhead
rolled for their bellies to be scratched.

Robbing Clam Beds

I wanted to get back on the water
and fly down the harbor
to my slip, eyes slit in windburn,
hair blown to a kingfisher's crest,
my skiff skipping waves
for the daughters of tourists
lined up on the pier,
not to straighten from the rake
to a woolpack fog rolling in
over the boat. But I had been
thinking about the secret cemetery
loving-places, or a dune cottage
on the gunnels, where each step
could be a walk out a window
or into a shoal of bluefish
the first rule of thumb
out there: Never think any deeper
than mud; when bluffs
over the water pale at the drowned
sun, you have minutes to get going
before you're circling in landless
murk. Which is where I tore
the motor's shear pin gunning it
over a rock, and began wishing
as I rowed toward either open sea
or the shelf ringing the island
that it was me Sgt. Hoppy
wanted to put the cuffs on, me
Judge Snow told to enlist

because of certain under-the-table
shellfish deals. I was willing
to be guilty of anything
so long as it happened on land,
not on this sandbar I found
by going over the side with both hands
on the gunnels, where each step
could be a walk out a window
or into a shoal of bluefish
that might dress me down to zero
in hungry August, and take all of me
south except the bones. Any minute
I'd wake in the back seat of somebody's
top-down Red Bitch Pontiac,
up a sand road deep in pineys,
far from Hoppy's cruiser flicking
black and white between the trees,
no longer a kid leaning into a rope,
hauling skiff, oars, motor, bagged clams
and all like one of those schoolbook
slaves who groaned the pyramid blocks
into place, except overseen by
a finger of shark-fear
pressing between my shoulders
and a god's razor over my skull
each time minnows flipped close.

Greenhorns

My mother settled on Charity,
I have returned here
to Half Moon Alley, to sit
perplexed with other men and boys
among chimneys cold as stones
arranged on a field to mark
immigrant suns and moons. Most of us
seem tranced, and stare
at far elevations whose names
we don't yet know
we will change to Hungry Hill,
Little Rome, and, after the Labor
Riots of '82, Vinegar Hill —
but now, in the moment before
dispersal, when some sit
back-to-back like Janus figures
guarding a holy well
in our Old Country, we don't
yet think of this as
the beginning. One who loves
a story, and looks monkey enough
to have modeled for cartoons
in a Yankee hate-sheet, will tell how
the light of Half Moon Alley
was seen in Portland, how someone
on the South Shore snatched a fifty
as it dropped flaming
down the air, though no man here
could describe a bill
of that unearthly figure. Others
speculate on how it began.
A landlord, or else a drunken
sleeper, his clay pipe's fireling
spilled on a rag mattress,
putting an end for now to the rat's
power; that and how fire companies
reined their horses in and went
light on the water. Cobbles
at my boots seem to emerge from dust

like ancestral skulls, and trying
to cancel that, I dream back to
a place where the raggedest crow
cries from the branch closest
to extinction. Soon I'll rise
and go, and in time appear
on the seats of drays and with
a watchman's lantern at India Wharf.
I'll ring a kind of shovel music
from curbs around a hydrant
on Louisburg Square, and help
the Statehouse grow wings. When
I'm called Gentleman Jim, I will
part my chamber's supplicants
with a boutonniere red as this city's seal.

Workout

I haven't laughed
at his cricket batsman's cap
since the first day he stepped out
on that deck, in seersucker pants,
wrists and neck buttoned,
and aligned his feet
as in a recollected bowling stance.
All over town men his age
are carving houses full of
minuscule furniture, or painting
every barb of every feather
on more-than-lifesize Canada geese,
and he could be locked in
all day talking to the cat
or waiting at table for anything
to happen. He steps off, lifting
out of eight decades one foot
at a time, fists churning
like a shadowboxer's.
It looks like sprinting under water,
the way he runs down
just in time for the far
railing and waits for breath
to catch up. Feeling
his way back along shingles,
his hands fend the house off.
He understands what, given time,
we all learn: teeth are temporary
and speed is relative to the air's
private resistance and the personal
pull of gravity. He begins again,
knowing not enough steps taken
often enough could end him at the P.O.
shirtless, in shorts, under
a campaign hat banded with safety pins.

The Last Man In The Quabbin

When I heard R. Dobson Moulton
in the post office, running off
about how, when the river rose
back of the new dams, there'd be
this three-toed claw of water
as if Eminent Domain was a great bird
that had stepped a foot smack down
and gouged three insignificant counties
from Enfield at the heel
way north to beyond Thompson Pond,
and how Mts. Zion and Ram
would be humped islands
neither man nor dog would run a deer on
again, it flushed a streak
in me I've had since boyhood.
You might remember me
if you drove a team too fast
up through town while I was crossing
the road to Woods' store.
I'd never move, but held my ground,
fists bunched, so you'd
have to choose: swerve
or cut me down quick as a weed.
Well, that morning
I made up my mind. I'd seen
those State boys disentrain
at Enfield summers ago, abristle
with charts and transoms,
and disappear into these hills,
traveling like rumors.
Sometimes they'd be in Packardsville,
then over to North Dana
and up by Warner Pond at the same time,
like they were ghosts
or maybe there were more of them
than any one person could see all at once.
Everyone and everything would go,
Moulton said, and the young orchards
breed back to wildness as though
time could run in reverse.
When I saw old Harry Larkin

weeping like a baby under his well porch
while a bulldozer plowed
his house and buildings in,
it hit to home. Those years
there were houses on the roads
going everywhere, trucked out on blocks,
sold off for less than a hundred dollar bill.
The railroad went like a carpet,
or matchsticks after a game of cards,
they just come along it and pulled
the ties up after them, and from Mt. Ram
there were all these
broccoli-looking clumps
where the oak groves were laid over.
By August 1, all from the four towns
were to be out of the valley,
and guards posted, but there must have been
something of the twist of Daniel Shays
in me, maybe from twenty years
of chasing up and down his same hills,
and I wasn't leaving for any bolt factory
in Springfield, or to occupy
a back room down to Worcester
like some widow's star boarder. I had
no wife and children, just my home place,
which I'd as soon sell
as put up with nightly powwows
with my father's ghost for doing so.
Let the Boss-tonians take it.
Then I thought, No, I will fix things
to suit myself. Rifle, axe, whetstone,
winter clothes and shoes, I made a list,
taking the whole of July
to figure everything I'd need.
I had no work. I run a garage
out on the Monson Turnpike
till one by one customers dropped away
like leaves, and I closed her.
I knew a cave, way up on Zion,
maybe the same one where old Glazier Wheeler
minted silver coins, as the story

has it, because a hollow tree
serves as the smoke hole. I ran across it
hunting coon one season.
Meanwhile the good ladies of Greenwich
were penning sad goodbyes
in the rhythms of "Hiawatha,"
and the Commonwealth was torching everything
it couldn't sell nor steal. Houses,
timber slash, whatever fire would take to.
The golf course and railroad
was paid in full, of course, and the full moon
of July rose through that smoke
orange as at harvest, but the only crops here
were people and their places, under
the leased blades of the engineers.
Those nights I used that moon
to cross the plain to Zion,
laden with things checked off my list,
even the front door and its frame, one night,
which I re-hung in the cave mouth,
fitting the edges tight with stone and mortar.
They say that cemetery
where my people were resettled
looks like a city park. I'll never know.
I know how towns look, empty,
as if gold or oil had brought the living
there and then played out.
Only the stones remained,
waiting for water to soften their edges,
and not one bird would cross the air
over that no-man's land. One night
I piled heaps of rags,
torn shirts and such, about
the barn and house, and soaked the hay,
shaking the kerosene jug
near to dry. Then I just walked
around the place, scratching
kitchen matches on my seat,
pouring tears for all my people's
sweat. I wasn't eating honey,
I can tell you. I was the only creature

moving on that plain, and partway
across I looked back, though I'd said
I mustn't, but couldn't tell my fire
from a score of others. I swore
I wouldn't go back. I have though,
when the ice around this island
thickens enough, and there's no snow
or the way's not deep, sometimes
I cross. I think of it as
"going to Massachusetts," and follow
a wall uphill till I come to the bar way
where pa's gate has fallen in,
or been broken down by hikers.
The cellar's there, still chuck-a-block
with char, though red pine's
climbed in from the pasture,
and the six sugar maples in the dooryard
have seeded children.
From a ledge on Zion I watched
the water back up, at first like heat ripples
down valley; then mill ponds
that used to be back of towns ran over
and spread, and the Swift River kept
thickening its silver. Riddles of water
everywhere, but it took years of snowmelt
roaring down defiles and over inclines
wide as the Monson Turnpike
to cover snips of road that began and ended
nowhere or drove up to a cellar hole
and curved away from disgust or chagrin.
Me, I'm just some hairy joe
in a smoke-smelly mackinaw
you meet among the trees but don't
get close to. I might have more than
buttons missing. I might even live
somewhere near here, but if asked
I'll only vary the old punchline:
You can't get there from anywhere.
Whatever I dump into this reservoir
comes out the end of a Boston faucet.

Ghosting

Thick of fog. No east-leaning point
of fir trees, no dove to send forth,
and no good to shoot your mouth off
in screams the fog will muffle
easier than bullets caught
in a ballistics box. Row steadily
into a slow beat, and don't accuse
yourself of anything just now,
or trust your eyes — they want to see
suns like flitches of bleached straw
working through everywhere.
Nowhere means disconnection, means
out here, but here there are islands,
each with its own rote, depending
how ocean falls on which kind of shore,
and there's sniffing the air
and listening, but not for voices.
When you hear baby talk it is only
water stirred by your oar tips,
not that you're shrinking back to
helplessness. Trust evergreen smells
for landfall, but not with the reek
of guano and flocks *gleeing* — that
means the Gannet Walls, surf bashing,
a ninth wave and a hard place.
Let fog enter your mind just enough
to erase such images, as well as
your inner map of this bay,
which by now is both crumpled
and stretched out of shape. So as not
to be fooled if a one-lunger begins
stroking nearby, someone out checking
his pots, learn your body's thudding
by heart. Pine smoke, like music,
can be trailed back to a door

on Green Point, and a grease-pit whiff of
route 1A over a slosh of gravel
or surf rattling egg-stones
means those Wash-ashores barbecuing
over on Little Sister, who wouldn't
mind today if you came from nowhere
through rib and burger fumes to wring
the pints in your watch cap
all over their patio.

Summer School

Three coke bottles of your Uncle Sal's
homemade red couldn't give me back
summer, 1958, and the one glance
it took in Organic lab to scramble
my ketones with my aldehydes —
it was a little *mal occhio*, a little bit
French nun, and you were that dark
woman the disabled give up their
subway seats for, the kind
a grown man looks at only once, and
even at mass takes on the instant,
permanent face of loss for.
In your mother's living room, behind
your father's garage, barefoot on
evening grass where insects zigging
too near our colliding particles
crackled and burned out, kissing you
was like sampling a little of everything
your *nonni* devised in her summer kitchen
below the stairs. Those nights
I stumbled home through the changed
streets, drunk on your breath
and mumbling in tongues, saying
Cassata alla Siciliana, Pasticcio,
Zuppa di Vongoli, to lean on the back door
humming and sweating like a nervous
frigidaire, finally understanding
how your cousins might be driven
to slaughter each other in Fanotti's
and the Old Palermo, and not so much
elevating you to a pedestal
as onto the shoulders of six fishermen
to be borne through streets
where I'd pin on you
the petitions of a towering desire.
Fireworks; hangdog days spreading with

humid silences; hour of the graven
forehead and your veal marsala
arrested a moment on your mother's
screen door, a chic wall hanging.
Had we kissed just then, with that
metal between us, it would have run like
mercury through our fingers. What's worse,
Sicilian Muse, I knew you knew.

The Knot Hole Gang

DeMarco said the special bus
from Braves' Field would pick us up
at a park way across town, a red bus
with an Indian's head on the front
just like the one on the nickel
it took to admit us to the bleachers,
and he led the way
to a mange of dust and grass
an hour from home, named for a war hero,
with its swings knotted irrevocably
and one kid who stayed
behind the chain link fence and said,
"Hey kid, it ain't gonna come,"
over and over till Marchant
chased him with a bat.
Somebody shouted "Here it comes!"
every time a truck
backfired out on the parkway,
and if you had driven by on your way
to the track and seen us there,
you might have thought how American
we were in our baseball caps,
with gloves the size of bushel baskets
on our belts, their palms thumped
black, with smiles torn out
at our knees and our ankles bulging
the rubber discs on those Keds
that each spring made teachers throw
all the windows open and beg us
never to wear them to school again,
with our lunch bags sweating
sandwich oils through the long afternoon.

Your New Dog

Call him whatever will testify
to the way he'll sight up trees
after squirrels, or to how
he'll sleep on his back,
legs wide, exposing himself to
the children's disgust.
Think of him living at seven times
your speed, yet never asking
if he's happy, then name him
someone who'll keep the beast in you
alive, who occasionally breaks
your commandments, and has to be
bailed out of the pound.
A dog who lifts tennis balls
from the court up the road,
and appears to wish his mouth
so capacious that he could divulge
them all, one at a time, the way
a magician produces eggs.
He's the one who'll take off
on rabbit tangents, and disappear
to rake blueberries off a bush,
purpling his teeth,
teeth he'll expose in a shame-face
to confess he's been sleeping
on the couch while you were out.
Loving what death can touch,
let that tail plume
waving without constraint
above the grasshead level of the field
teach you the pleasures of
the instant. Then, when you hold
each other and howl, any theologian
who denies your dog a soul
will feel his eyes
involuntarily roll up inside his head.

Those Times

There are times when you see
farthest, beyond currents,
splashes, waves of grass
that mimic tides the field
suffers at flood,

to the brown fringe before
Try Island, outskirts
of awareness where you're
watched by many eyes:
whimbrels, frozen in profile
midstride, looking
woven of sunburnt grass.

More and more those times
are when the best things
happen, but you can't
live there; waking, can't
keep a Chinese ideogram
freestanding out the window,
black strokes on whiteness
like an oriental gateway
you might translate,

"This is the happiness
of four a.m., the second
before the mind engages
itself and the page turns
moonlight, the brush-swipes
only the crown of a pine."

Looking For Captain Teabag

At your car's first crunch on
the clamshell road, breeds
you might like to see
under different circumstances

arraign themselves: Rin-tin-beagle,
fender thumpers, tire-chewers
limber as spider monkeys,
a leaping chowhound.

Were you expecting salukis
and widow's walks here in Dogtown?
This neighborhood floated over
in the thirties, just before
the island went under, the houses barged
when tides got too close too often.

Grade school versions of home,
they look planted where they washed up;
painted out of assorted buckets, nothing
fits together, half that one
goes with half that one over there

because, in the high-stakes winter games
of legend, you could ante up with anything
from an ell to your whole place.

Tar paper, tin chimneys patched
with coffee cans, a rusty kettle
flue cap: the unexamined life, no names
or numbers and nobody home — anonymity

against repossession — and the dogs out front,
or wolverines tied with pack thread,
can smell a summons before it leaves
the courthouse. In town they said

for lobsters see Captain Teabag,
out the Dogtown road. They might
have sent you here for Uncle Junior

or The Shingler, whoever stole
the Evinrude off your transom
or the cord of wood he sold you,
or is building a new garage
with the lumber for your new garage.

Were you expecting gold buttons on
a navy background? Down there at the end,
in green workclothes, among crowbarred
draggers run up in the grass

around the creek, there in the shadows
pooled under the deep horseshoe curves
of their bows. "Are you Captain Teabag?"

He seems jumpy, tilting a bit, as though
on a short leg. And now, while seas
shift behind his eyes, flats and tides
rearranging themselves —

Don't get out! A mongrel cloud of
barbershop sweepings gets up and circles
itself like the local gene pool,
and your man says, "My name is Alton P. Snow."

Light From Fundy

All night a wind
drawing cold off the water's
basins and swells,
herding aluminum chairs
to a corner of the porch,

until one's ghostly rocking
drew me to moonlight
to see whether an old owner
of the land hadn't returned
to find how it's doing
without his cows
to graze seedlings off.

There was only the apples'
underleaf, turned up,
a white light laundering
toward snowblindness,

and the *putsch, putsch,*
of flowerpots toppling
one by one off the rail —
the wind's sharpshooting.

This morning, in among
raspberry canes, I found
the last of that light,
like a filtrate

of our pine-winy air,
thinner, above last year's
leaves, in the first place
fall appears.

Whirl Is King

Here and there
in the trees' understories,
that momentary thumbling's piping out
a helix of song

palpable as zebraic
black-and-white warblers
who tailgate each other,
running the bugs down, though

it's not one of them
or even a redstart
or parula that's
picked its way here

across consecutive dusks,
barely ahead of the air's
polar bulge. My eyes
dive through binoculars

till dimensions queue up,
then back off to focus
in time for a branch's
empty trembling. There

it is again. Be quick,
be quick, quicker than
the way one chickadee
appears to become two

who dive to admit
a third and suddenly
all change to a treeful of
olive-feathered fingerlings,

air-fish off in a single
upswing so I turn in a vortex
of my own, grabbing the rail
just before the misstep.

Listening To September

In this season of brief arrivals
and long departures,
when light and shade meander
through these pines
slow as Holsteins, I spend
an afternoon turning things
upside down to see whether
arrowheads or train-flattened
pennies fall out. Those new
whistlers back there in the trees
sound like kids calling a dog
in their private way,
though I know they are only
birds, or only memory
like time burrowing in
ledge over ledge, dovetailing,
holding on. When they were kids,
men I used to know
herded cows here, after
the oaks fell for ships and
their business, before pines
parceled the river out
to pools backing their stands.
No houses this side, only
treeless pasture then,
and though those whistlers
may be warblers I've never seen,
passing through, I don't
want to spot them
for my list just now.

Fall Squashes

The lettuce long bolted to exotic
headdresses, beanleaf riddled to ribs,
I find them beneath tatterdemalion
leaves: little exclamations,
not the bludgeons of August
left on friends' carseats,
but the plants' final nudges,
green and gold, and patty pans
like the minor gears of some natural
machine — which I brush with garlic oil
and grill briefly, and eat for
themselves alone. Tasting how well
they've survived root borers and slugs,
days of blue, unmoving air,
I think back along the vine
to the first watermelon-tigered leaf,
the seed-shell riding its edge,
and beyond to the flat seed
with its journey packed in,
as deep as anything.

Willow, Wishbone, Warblers

The way this willow traps
fallen branches till it looks like
a collapsed rookery,
and keeps sun out of this room,

and taps the vegetables' water,
fattening on vitamins
so it's taller than the house now,
and, come March, won't put out

many catkins — but for the enchantment
of a single branch bobbing on air
after some winged departure,
I'd take a saw to it.

The trunk and limbs would make fenceposts
for the garden, or in the fireplace
hold off a few winter evenings,
and the branches could supply

years of beanpoles tall enough
so the tendrils could work out
any Book of Kells design they had
in mind. Mainly it's the birds, though,

all those minute fussings in its
leaves, calls and their seedy replies,
convincing me, August through September,
that I'm simpler than I think,

a gawper at flutterings down the trunk
though I've vowed to lock up
the field glasses, not to look this year
when immature warblers that won't stay put

long enough to be anything
run their mirroring duets like air shows
around the trees, and far out on the bay,
flocks go stringing over water

in lines that falter and break to flecks
and lift again on their wishbones
beyond all but a suggestion of birds
backlit by evening, beyond even

my intuition of their cries, and I praise
the fact beneath superstition's skin:
that bone we go dowsing for luck with,
there like a small horseshoe stamped in.

Black Bear In October

From yesterday's feed of boozy
windfall mash
all the way back
to the first crunched leaflets of
jack-in-the-pulpit,
the year's a blurred ramble,

a hand-to-mouth wandering
from hives smashed like pinatas
to gardens where squash vines,
anxious to push out
the last of their litters, turned
all elbows and knees.

Midsummer naps were as long
as it takes stones to give up sunlight,
not like this sleep she's just
hauled herself from,

in this hill orchard
where low, fast flights
seem to be going the wrong way,
and higher up, out of focus,
each wing lope
is cried out on the air.

There were hints,
if she'd cared enough
to stop dragging chokecherries
off a bush: that gold foil panic
in the trees,

and that moment the air
went acute,
when every tendril sensed fall
and turned its barb
back on itself.

Among leaves strewn
like parings of Golden Delicious,
she fights a mantle of fat
that's weighing her
into whitening grass,
groans amazement to find herself
quilled with frost.

October Flocks

Not a starry ball of land birds
drifting and lazing, rolling above trees,
wowing from time to time into
starbursts, then drawing in,
centripetal,
and spinning off around
a central torque,
but shore birds far out over windless water,
forty miles from mainland.

They made no sound,
though all the time they passed,
sky-wide, I heard
one of the shuddering engines
of the planet
beating on without uncertainty,

the shifting center invisible
but somehow there inside
the whole, where single lines
dashed and sprinted into
the group's dissolve,

clots and strayings on the sky,
single offshootings, a momentary
falling out —
how many second winds
between Labrador and here?

Creation: a coercion out of nothing.
Out of nowhere gone into nowhere
in minutes, instinct's energy
spending in the dark muscle
over each sternum
enough to turn the earth.

Pole Beans

Bed is right, the way
I tucked seed into mounds
and in a few days
they sat up, seeming to rub
sleep from their new faces,

and later opened
little getaway wings,
then threw grappling arms
around poles to rise,
hanging on until

they could raise themselves
a few days higher
into fog, considering droplets
as the mind examines ideas,
aspiring over their heads

even as I tore creeping
indolence out, and the other
weeds, and deflated slugs
who gorged on them
like bad habits.

And so, having started them
on their way, and regretting
I have to leave them
to everything that
noses through the dark,

I will rig up the guidelines
whereby they get a chance
to scrawl signatures
on the air, and pretend
fatherly surprise at their
blue outbursts,

and remove whatever swells
under their green hearts
until one night the snow
turns them sepia — handwriting
over the backs of old photographs.

Cougar

Non-native plantings stuck into lawns,
welded chain supporting the mailboxes,
too many electives at the regional
school — we were in danger
until a state trooper saw it
pad with dignity across the road
in his headlights, and the dark
around here became furred
with something more than frost.
Some are betting that it's
what jumps electric fence
to ride pigs bareback, going for
the neck, digging in along the flanks,
printing a five-foot stride,
and that it's wearing a collar
because a camper let it out
when it got too big for his van,
but nobody's playing expert
with this mystery, though
they're reaching back for stories.
Good to know we have places
the houselights don't pin down,
so the slick-magazine man from Boston
can stop speculating about
our drinking habits; good to feel,
going from car to porchlight,
the short hairs lifting off my neck.

Weather Breeder

This heron-still day,
clipped from April
and stuck upsidedown
on the January page,
is a trick. The calendar
should be fretted, torn,
and flung at every window,
but sky and bay
appear to have changed
places, the water so flat
and full it looks
tideless, as if we could
walk it to Chapman's Cove,
past undissolved rings
from a loon's dive,
and a raft of buffleheads
drifting in flight pattern
under clouds like sepias
of combers. This is
the second trick, and
the third's how we'll pay
come April — in this day's
place, the wind offshore
veering around East,
with gulls huddled in
the least backwaters, facing
up to the long fetch of air.

Nests

On a flat midweek morning
we take down the soap-bottle
angel with one wrong eye,
the reindeer clothespins whose racks
were pipecleaners, everything
teachers believe salvageable,
as if Christmas celebrated a world
redeemed from dumpkeepers.
Truth is that in the end
that tree I waded wiry scrub for —
and sawed between passing headlights,
crouched as though placating
some hairy pantheist squatting
in the blood — had seemed to crowd out
of its corner, cornering us
as if the branches still pushed
themselves into the room
on what little water the stand
cupped. A northern tribe,
we can't sustain our holidays.
Work the world exacts
cries out to be done: octagonal,
eggshell-empty things hung
against darkness have to be nested
in eight-sided holes, everything
wrapped and boxed and the tree
left for quail cover,
a few strands of tinsel clinging
in the hope a bird might weave one
into a future construction,
as occasionally they do.

Beachplums

A morning storm tosses at the windows
like certain blossoms I know,
and I hold a ruby jar to my eye.
May this be a good year for them,
in spring darkness the roadsides
banked so with blossoms you might think
the plow had just passed.
Then, in latest August we'll check
our places between the bike trail
and Hatch's Harbor, where wind
has worked the dunes to a making sea
alchemized into sand. Doubled over,
fighting inclines that fill our shoes,
we'll go for crowning green
where heat has simmered the berries
through yellow to deep red, blue,
purple, all with a salt patina
that takes our fingerprints. Reaching
for undersides, we'll take care for
poison ivy and whatever else, though
all that usually blows up there
are a few horned larks breaking cover.
I'll slap myself against horsefly
or bee when the first sweat bead
forms on my nape, and remember
five-dollar bushels I sold to buy
school shoes, thirty and more
years ago. For blue- and huckleberries,
July and August; but these at the year's
apex, before the unleafing slide into snow.
We'll pick till we're almost too dry
to carry the doubled, twenty-pound bags
home, and there pick again for stems
and leaves, allowing a few yellow
and green berries in the stewpot for
pectin. For straining, I'll donate
a t-shirt. Boiled with equal sugar

till a few drops run together and don't
fall off the spoon, the liquid jells.
Then layers of paraffin, ladled gently
over the full jars, being sure
to seal the edges. Deep in January
I hold a jar like a votive candle
and pop the cap and wafer of wax,
inhaling a little sun returned from
numberless dune facets, and a little spray.
Beyond wavering light, the sea
at Stellwagen Bank comes forward a little.

Stone Arabia Farm

This upstate air is open steelwork,
like the bridge over the river
where dead water's still withdrawing stones
from a millrun they named after the town
and tribe. When strangers come
they scavenge brick and cast iron for
their patios; nobody stays to see how old
old wood gets. Call this place "convenient
to Thruway," and the farm "a handyman's
dream," though it's only a monument
to sucker punches and jacked deer.
We push the kitchen door to, hunch in
under a ceiling bellying its laths.
Dishes frozen upright in the pan
parody those Turners on the hill,
their slates ringed by wrought iron.
Goodbye is on the table in blue crayon,
a touch of the gift to be simple, though
shattered gun racks spell hurry correctly.
One wild root since Ticonderoga, they went
wherever their name would still
admit them. A slush of ice
thickens up pipes to house stroke.
No need to come here anymore, unless
you've quit the school named for the street
named for the hardware king, and need a target.
"Barn for dressage, needs someone with
imagination." Read: somebody who sees eaves
hung with perfect ice, whose wrapping-paper
mind will paint watercolor cardinals
fat and flocked like pigeons, someone
who'll believe the boy
who'll swear he bought that evergreen
he's dragging home through snow.

Seals In The Inner Harbor

Ducks, at first, except they didn't
fly when we rounded the jetty
and swung into the channel,
didn't spread panic among themselves,
peeling the whole flock off the water,
but followed, popping under
and poking up as if to study our faces
for someone, their eyes rounded still
by the first spearing shock of ice,
or amazed to find our white town
here again, backed by a steeple
telling the hours in sea time.
Their skeptical brows seemed from a day
when men said a green Christmas
would fill this harbor with dead
by February. We left them hanging
astern at world's edge, afloat on
summer's afterlife: gray jetty,
water and sky, the one gray vertical
of smoke rising straight from a chimney
across the cove. We could believe
they were men who had dragged
this bottom till its shells were smooth
and round as gift shop wampum,
who never tied up and walked away
a final time, but returned for evenings
like this was going to be, thirsting
for something to fight salt off with,
needing a place to spit and plan
the rescue of children's children.